Native American
Family Life

COLLEEN MADONNA FLOOD WILLIAMS

Senior Consulting Editor Dr. Troy Johnson
Professor of History and American Indian Studies
California State University

MASON CREST PUBLISHERS • PHILADELPHIA

NATIVE AMERICAN LIFE

NATIVE AMERICAN LIFE

Native American
Family Life

COLLEEN MADONNA FLOOD WILLIAMS

Senior Consulting Editor Dr. Troy Johnson
Professor of History and American Indian Studies
California State University

MASON CREST PUBLISHERS • PHILADELPHIA

As always, to Paul R. Williams and Dillon J. Meehan
with all my love. Especially for Kayleigh and Michael Baker
and for Mathew and Maureen.

Mason Crest Publishers
370 Reed Road
Broomall PA 19008
www.masoncrest.com

First printing

1 3 5 7 9 8 6 4 2

Library of Congress Cataloging-in-Publication Data
on file at the Library of Congress

ISBN 1-59084-126-3

Table of Contents

Introduction

For hundreds of years the dominant image of the Native American has been that of a stoic warrior, often wearing a full-length eagle feather headdress, riding a horse in pursuit of the buffalo, or perhaps surrounding some unfortunate wagon train filled with innocent west-bound American settlers. Unfortunately there has been little written or made available to the general public to dispel this erroneous generalization. This misrepresentation has resulted in an image of native people that has been translated into books, movies, and television programs that have done little to look deeply into the native worldview, cosmology, and daily life. Not until the 1990 movie *Dances with Wolves* were native people portrayed as having a human persona. For the first time, native people could express humor, sorrow, love, hate, peace, and warfare. For the first time native people could express themselves in words other than "ugh" or "Yes, Kemo Sabe." This series has been written to provide a more accurate and encompassing journey into the world of the Native Americans.

When studying the native world of the Americas, it is extremely important to understand that there are few "universals" that apply across tribal boundaries. With over 500 nations and 300 language groups the worlds of the Native Americans were diverse. The traditions of one group may or may not have been shared by neighboring groups. Sports, games, dance, subsistence patterns, clothing, and religion differed—greatly in some instances. And although nearly all native groups observed festivals and ceremonies necessary to insure the renewal of their worlds, these too varied greatly.

Of equal importance to the breaking down of old myopic and stereotypic images is that the authors in this series credit Native

Americans with a sense of agency. Contrary to the views held by the Europeans who came to North and South America and established the United States, Canada, Mexico, and other nations, some Native American tribes had sophisticated political and governing structures—that of the member nations of the Iroquois League, for example. Europeans at first denied that native people had religions but rather "worshiped the devil," and demanded that Native Americans abandon their religions for the Christian worldview. The readers of this series will learn that native people had well-established religions, led by both men and women, long before the European invasion began in the 16th and 17th centuries.

Gender roles also come under scrutiny in this series. European settlers in the northeastern area of the present-day United States found it appalling that native women were "treated as drudges" and forced to do the men's work in the agricultural fields. They failed to understand, as the reader will see, that among this group the women owned the fields and scheduled the harvests. Europeans also failed to understand that Iroquois men were diplomats and controlled over one million square miles of fur-trapping area. While Iroquois men sat at the governing council, Iroquois clan matrons caucused with tribal members and told the men how to vote.

These are small examples of the material contained in this important series. The reader is encouraged to use the extended bibliographies provided with each book to expand his or her area of specific interest.

Dr. Troy Johnson
Professor of History and American Indian Studies
California State University

1 Native American Families

Families are the building blocks of society. Thus, it is no wonder that Native American societies of the past and present revolve around the family. Traditionally, Native American family ties are traced through blood relationships, *clans*, bands, and tribes. Sometimes, adoptions establish family ties.

The varying family structures of Native Americans are quite complex. There are nuclear and extended Native American families. A nuclear family, or one generational family, is composed of a mother, father, and their children. An extended family is composed of two or more generations of a family living together.

This Native American family is dressed in traditional clothing, called regalia, which is worn for special occasions or tribal ceremonies. Family relationships are very important to Native Americans, and social life often revolves around the family.

Clans are another form of Native American families. A *totem* or a common ancestor generally links a clan. Clan traditions, customs, and organizational patterns vary greatly from region to region and people to people.

This photograph from the 19th century shows a Native American family of the Plains outside of their home.

Obviously, Native American family life is a broad and complicated subject. The following chapters of this book will look at some of the different aspects of the family lifestyles of select groups of pre-Columbian and early-contact Native American cultures. These groups have been chosen to provide a representation of the differing lifestyles of pre-Columbian and early-contact Native American families throughout the Americas.

In this book, the past tense is used not to suggest that Native American families are a thing of the past. It is used solely to signify that these family descriptions are referring to Native American families from pre-European contact to early-European contact periods.

To learn more about Native American families, the author recommends that you study in greater depth the family structures, traditions, and customs of individual tribes. Keep in mind that no two families are exactly alike. This applies to Native American families, just as it does to all other families. It is important to note that while the families of the cultural regions depicted in this book shared many things in common, they were also vastly different in many ways. ᔕ

11

A shaman wearing a mask peers through the doorway of an
Iroquois longhouse. When the first French and English settlers
arrived in northeastern North America during the early 17th
century the Iroquois Nation—actually a group of tribes that
included the Onondaga, Mohawk, Seneca, Oneida, Cayuga,
and Tuscarora tribes—controlled much of the region.

2 The Iroquois Family of Nations

The Haudenosaunee (Iroquois) people envisioned themselves as being one giant family. In fact, they formed a family of nations. The name, Haudenosaunee, which is used to refer to this Iroquoian nation, means, "People of the Longhouse." The symbolic *longhouse* they shared was the northeast woodlands. The Mohawk were the Guardians of the Eastern Door of the Haudenosaunee's great figurative longhouse. The Seneca were the Guardians of the Western Door. *Lineage* was traced through the maternal, or mother's side, of the longhouse family.

In descriptions of their large, extended family, the Haudenosaunee referred to the tribes within their nation as brothers. The Elder Brothers of the Haudenosaunee are the Onundagaono (Onondaga), Kanienkahagen (Mohawk), and Onondowahgah (Seneca). The Younger Brothers are the Onayotekaono (Oneida), Guyohkohnyoh (Cayuga), and Ska-Ruh-Reh (Tuscarora).

The Haudenosaunee taught their children to respect and honor both their younger and elder brother tribes. They also taught their children to be thankful for their "Three Sisters"—corn, squash, and beans. These three important food staples supported, sustained, and nurtured the growth of the Haudenosaunee nation.

Iroquois children inherited the clan symbol and ties of their mother. When a man and a woman married, the man moved from his mother's longhouse to the longhouse of his wife. He owned only personal items, clothing, and weapons.

The true center of longhouse family relationships revolved around the fireside family. A fireside family, like a nuclear family, was made up of a mother, a father, and their children. The Iroquois family then branched out to include extended family or clan members. Tribal nationality was comprised of clans. Finally, the intertribal family of the nation was made up of the members of all of its smaller tribes, bands, or "brother" nations.

Another group of Native Americans that lived on the Atlantic Coast of North America was the Algonquians. The members of the Algonquian-language family formed alliances similar to the Iroquois Confederacy. However, these alliances were never as structured as that of the Haudenosaunees. They tended to be looser groupings of small bands of Algonquian peoples that joined together only during battle or to trade with one another.

Grand sachems, or chiefs, led Algonquian bands joined together as confederacies. The lesser chiefs of the individual tribal bands were known as *sagamores*. The grand sachems often served as negotiators for the sagamores. Algonquian tribes were often *matrilineal*; however, some, like the Mi'kmaq, were *patrilineal*.

Daily work was divided between the two *moieties* of a clan. When a member of one moiety died, the members of the other moiety would take care of the chores associated with the death of a family

A group of Native American boys practice with bows and arrows. In Iroquois tribes, boys learned archery and other hunting skills at a young age. This training would serve them well when they became adults, and therefore responsible for providing food for their family.

15

member. This allowed the deceased person's immediate moiety members to attend solely to their mourning.

Throughout the Northeast, women did the cooking, raised the children, and cared for the elderly members of their tribes. They did the weaving, tanning, pottery, and basket making. Women also made footwear and clothing for their families.

Women made cradleboards to make carrying their babies as they worked easier. The cradleboards were often decorated with ornate designs. Relatives and friends gave the woman special totems to hang from her child's cradleboard. This was done in order to help keep the baby healthy and safe.

These small figures depict a Native American storyteller entertaining a group of young listeners. Storytelling was a popular pastime among the Native Americans of the northeast. Both the adult figure and the young girl to the right are holding infant children in cradleboards.

Northeastern mothers often bathed their children in cold lakes and streams. This was believed to be necessary to help ensure a young child's survival through his or her first winter. The woodlands

The Mi'kmaq decorated their clothing with their clan symbol. They also painted it on their canoes, snowshoes, and other possessions.

could be a cold and harsh place to live during the winter. Young children needed to be **acclimated** to the cold. Being bathed in cold water helped to acclimate the young.

The Haudenosaunee women owned all property, and a respected elder matron led each family clan. Female clan leaders chose the sachems, or clan chiefs, for their tribes. If the woman who chose a sachem became displeased with the way he was representing their people, she could have him removed from his leadership position.

Haudenosaunee women were the keepers of the "Three Sisters." Mothers, daughters, and grandmothers sowed, tended, prayed over, and harvested the beans, squash, and corn that helped to feed their families. It was their responsibility to weed the fields and to store supplies of food for the family in underground caches.

The men of the Haudenosaunee nation hunted and trapped animals. They were brave warriors who protected their families and their nation. Haudenosaunee men were also responsible for making weapons and canoes. The clan sachems were men of the Haudenosaunee who represented their tribes at meetings of the Iroquois Confederacy. (If the men were from Algonquian tribes,

17

NATIVE AMERICAN LIFE

The majority of the Haudenosaunee were divided into three main clans: the turtle, bear, and wolf clans. Animals played an important role in Haudenosaunee spiritual life. A clan's totem animal was considered to be its kindred spirit. Animals were also often the main characters of religious and teaching stories told by the elders to the young.

then their sachems represented them at meetings of their own confederacies.)

Maternal uncles played an especially big role in the life of young male Haudenosaunees. Clans were linked through the mother's bloodlines, so a young man learned his family history from his mother's brothers. Maternal uncles were responsible for preparing their young nephews for clan life, important rituals, marriage, and the responsibilities of adult life.

Around the age of seven or eight, Haudenosaunee children were expected to begin performing chores. The chores that they were given helped ease the day-to-day workload of their fireside family. More importantly, the chores helped to prepare the children for their roles later on in life.

Young girls would help haul water and tend to the crops. They would also assist their mothers, aunts, and grandmothers with sewing and cooking. They learned to make clothing and footwear. They also learned to make cornhusk dolls and other toys for their younger siblings. Their aunts, grandmothers, and mothers shared stories and bits of wisdom with them as they worked. In this way, young girls gradually learned the skills necessary to be a responsible, productive wife and clan mother.

Haudenosaunee men were often away from home for long periods of time. Because of this, young boys were encouraged to "play" at fighting, hunting, and camping. This type of "play" helped them to learn important life skills.

Their mothers often made toy war clubs for them out of corn silk. The boys would use these soft clubs to participate in mock battles against their friends. This allowed them to learn important hand-to-hand combat skills.

To be capable providers and effective warriors, the young boys needed to perfect their use of snares, bow and arrows, blowguns, and other weapons. When their grandfathers, fathers, and uncles were home from hunting or war parties, the young boys learned how to make canoes, weapons, and tools. The elder men gave the younger men advice on how to become respected hunters, warriors, husbands, and fathers.

After a young boy killed his first deer, he was allowed to join the adult hunting parties. When he reached puberty, he was sent into the woods on a *vision quest*. A respected elder would often accompany the adolescent on this sacred journey.

At this time, the young man would demonstrate his physical strength, intelligence, and manliness. These were important assets, as life in the woodlands could be quite demanding. A young man would strive to demonstrate that he was capable of withstanding great challenges in order to protect and provide for his family and nation.

Around the year 1570, two influential men, Hiawatha and Deganawida, first encouraged the Cayuga, Mohawk, Oneida, Onondaga, and Seneca to unite. The Huron prophet Deganawida spoke of a vision of the tribes united beneath a "Great Tree of Peace." Hiawatha, a Mohawk medicine man, traveled by canoe throughout the Haudenosaunee territories speaking about the importance of unity.

Hiawatha and Deganawida's efforts were rewarded with the formation of the Iroquois Confederacy. This confederacy of tribes, or Iroquois nations, started out as a union of five nations. In the early 1700s, the Tuscarora joined the Haudenosaunee family of nations, bringing the number to six. Many historians now believe that the United States of America owes a debt of gratitude, not only to the Roman ideals of democracy and the republic, but also to the political models of the Haudenosaunee's Pine Tree Sachems, Grand Council, and Grand Council Fire.

The young man might also reveal his dreams to his elder companion. The elder would consider the young man's dreams carefully and identify the guardian spirit that was trying to show itself to the young man. The young man would then find or carve a symbol of that spirit to keep as a personal totem.

A young girl generally came of age around the same time that she became capable of bearing children. At this time, the girl's mother would build a small *wigwam* outside the main village. The girl would retreat into the wigwam for several days. She would pray for the blessings of healthy children, a good husband, and a long life. She would *fast* during this time, drinking only water.

Delaware boys participated in a coming-of-age initiation rite called the Youth's Vigil. A boy would enter the woods and fast for a number of days. Hopefully, he would have a vision during this time that revealed the spirit guides and forces that would protect and direct him from young manhood to old age.

For the Delaware tribe of the Algonquian people, marriage and divorce were simple matters. A man and woman who moved in together were considered to be husband and wife. If either one wanted a divorce, the man would leave the family dwelling. It was the wife's right to retain custody of the home and children.

Family life in the woodlands culture area was not all work. Although the children owned few possessions, their parents did make toys for them. Young girls and boys used sticks to roll hoops made out of birch bark along the ground. Animal skin balls were stuffed with feathers or fur. Men and boys played a demanding game, much like modern-day lacrosse, called baggataway.

Story telling was a favorite family activity that included young and old alike. The stories shared might be exciting, funny, scary, or sad. They were most certainly always entertaining, as the Haudenosaunee were known for their **oratorical** skills. Family elders used these stories to teach young people the secrets of successful living and the art of story telling, so that they might pass these things on to their own children. Ⴝ

21

NATIVE AMERICAN LIFE

A child watches from his position tied into
a cradleboard. Native American women
used the device to carry their children
while they worked at their daily chores:
planting and cultivating crops, preparing
meals, and making household items.

3 Parrots for Pets and Postball as a Pastime

In the region of the American South and the Caribbean Sea, clans were the most common family system. Among Native American tribes of the southeast, clans were mainly matrilineal. This was also the case with the Tainos, who lived in the Caribbean before arrival of Europeans in the late 15th century and early 16th century.

In the Caribbean, male rulers of Taino villages were known as caciques. If a female was the ruler of the village, she was called a cacias. The eldest son of the ruler's eldest sister traditionally succeeded a Taino leader. This practice made the Taino society primarily *patriarchal*, but also matrilineal.

During labor, a Southeastern woman often retreated to the privacy of a birthing hut. After the child was born, a ritual cleansing took place. Animal grease was rubbed all over the child's body and then the infant was placed in a cradleboard. Much of a child's first year of life would be spent in this cradleboard.

Southeastern women nursed their babies until they were about two years old. They were gentle mothers who did not often resort to physical punishments. More often than not, these wise mothers disciplined their children verbally. Good behavior was promoted through the use of high expectations, wit, and wisdom.

Mothers tried to instill the traits of humility, industriousness, common sense, and cool-headedness in the young women of their families, clans, or tribes. They did this through story telling, by being good role models, and by having their young girls assist them with the family chores.

Women did the planting, tended the gardens, and harvested the crops. Women made clothing for themselves, their husbands, and their children. They also made pottery, tanned animal skins, and wove fine baskets and mats. These skills were all patiently taught to their granddaughters, nieces, and daughters.

Women prepared the meals. Corn chowders, cornbreads, or some other corn dish was a part of almost every family meal. Family meals often featured wild game, such as bear, deer, fish, or turkey. Pumpkins, beans, peas, potatoes, and squash might also accompany such meats.

Taino women wove, made hammocks, cooked, and prepared the *cassava*. They also attended to their husbands' hair and painted their

A French explorer and artist named Jacques le Moyne was assigned the task of documenting the lifestyles and homes of the natives of Florida, as well as mapping the terrain. His journals and drawings have become an important historical resource on the Timucua people.

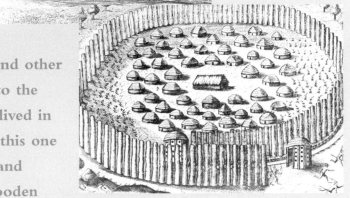

The Timucua and other Indians native to the Florida region lived in houses such as this one made of grass and reeds over a wooden framework. When the first Spanish explorers arrived in the region during the 16th century, they found many Timucua settlements. Some were walled, as in this drawing, to keep out enemy tribes or wild animals.

bodies according to ceremonial rules. If single, a women went without clothes; if married, she would wear a kind of apron that covered her from her waist to the middle of her legs.

Men were the family guardians and bravely protected their families and homes. They stood up for the rights of their family, both within their communities and within the world at large. They held the members of their family accountable for poor behavior, but also celebrated the

This 16th-century illustration by Jacques LeMoyne shows Taino natives paddling a dugout canoe. To make these canoes, the Taino cut down a large tree and hollowed it by using stone tools as well as careful applications of fire. Men used the canoes to hunt and fish.

achievements of their wives and children.

The men of the Southeast did the arduous work of clearing the fields so that the women could farm. Creek boys helped women in the gardens until they reached puberty. More often than not, however, men were usually off hunting, fighting, or fishing.

Many Southeastern men were permitted to have more than one wife. A good provider or a wealthy man might have as many wives as he could support. However, his first wife always retained her social status as being the first. Frequently, it was the right of a first wife to approve of or disapprove of her husband's choice of subsequent wives.

Timucua and other men of the Southeast often tattooed their bodies. A man's family status and skill as a warrior was often indicated through such tattoos. The Timucua would severely punish a man who tattooed

The name the Cherokee use for their people is Ani-Yun'Wiya. This means the "main people." The name "Cherokee" is thought to have come from a word used by the Choctaw to label the Ani-Yun'Wiya as "the people of the land of many caves."

himself with tattoos that reflected a higher status than he had truly earned. The offender was forced to remove the tattoos from his body.

Further south, in the Caribbean, the Taino men wore a *breechcloth* of cotton or palm fibers cut to a specific length to show rank. This made it easy for other members of his home and village to see his status among them.

Large groups of Taino men lived in houses called bohios. One bohio might house from 10 to 15 Taino men, as well as their entire families. It was not uncommon for a Taino bohio to serve as home to up to 100 people.

Taino men cleared the land so that their women could farm it. They hunted, fished, and made wooden dugout canoes. They used their canoes to hunt ducks and sea turtles.

Taino men trained dogs to assist them in their hunts. Taino men were peaceful and engaged in battle primarily only for self defense from the warrior Caribs that raided their villages.

The Carib men were known as fierce warriors. They traveled about the Caribbean, raiding the villages of neighboring communities.

27

NATIVE AMERICAN LIFE

They often took prisoners, and it is said that they were cannibals. Male prisoners would be eaten. Female prisoners became the wives or slaves of their captors. Carib men were also expert sailors and fishermen whose dugout canoes were sometimes fitted with sails.

Carib communities traced their relationships through matrilineal kin groups. They did not have chiefs. Carib wives were often women who had been taken from other island communities, like the Tainos, that the Carib had raided.

Children played together for the first few years of their lives. It was not unusual for children under four or five years of age to go without clothing during the warm months of spring and summer. Around five or six, children were expected to begin learning their respective life skills.

Boys learned from their uncles, fathers, and grandfathers. They had close relationships with their maternal uncles, who oversaw their growth from boys to men. Boys were taught how to fish, hunt, and trap. They learned how to make bows and arrows. They carved spears and clubs to be used in battle. They were taught how to clear the land for farming and how to build **palisades** to protect their villages.

In their spare time, when they weren't helping their families or their villages, boys learned to do fine carvings and make tobacco pipes and ceremonial drums. A top-quality drum, ornately carved war club, or a first-rate tobacco pipe was a treasured item. Skillful craftsmen who could make these types of items were held in high regard.

Women of the village trained young girls in the arts of weaving, sewing, cooking, courting, marriage, and motherhood. Grandmothers, aunts, and mothers all spoke to the girls about the qualities of a good wife and mother. They talked to the girls about traditional family values, religious beliefs, and acceptable social behavior.

The little girls watched, learned, and helped as their mothers and other women of the tribe made clothing and blankets. They learned to make pottery, sleeping mats and floor mats out of cane, and finely woven grass baskets. The girls were also taught to cook, dry, and store corn and other food staples.

The Caribs were a fierce people that lived in the Caribbean region. They often attacked the villages of other tribes, as this Theodore DeBry illustration of 1570 shows.

For many young women of the Southeast, coming of age meant starting their menstrual cycles. This great milestone in a young girl's life was marked by a special ceremony. At this time, young girls began to practice a ritual that they would observe monthly, until late in life when they reached menopause. The day their period began, they were separated from the rest of their family and village.

A hut was set aside to house a menstruating woman. She used this time to rest, pray, and meditate. When her period ended, she took a ritual cleansing bath. Afterwards, she would put on clean clothing and return to her family home.

There were many things that a young boy needed to know and do to become a man. His uncles, father, and grandfathers tried to help him understand his place in the family, community, and world at large. Young men in the Southeast were expected, in some tribes, to participate in a battle and prove their skill as warriors before they would be declared men. Other tribes dictated that a young man who wished to marry must build a home and kill a bear or a deer, proving to all that he could be a good provider. The transition from boyhood to manhood was always cause for great family celebration.

Marriage for the Seminoles was a fairly casual relationship. If a man wanted to divorce his wife, he merely left their home. Other Southeastern tribes planned arranged marriages for their children.

A series of talks would take place between the women of the two clans. They would let the fathers of both children know what was going on, but the men had no real influence in the matter. If the women decided it was a good match, the young girl would be asked if she would consent to the marriage.

Next, the girl would place a bowl of food outside her home. The young man who wished to marry her would ask if he might have a taste of the food. If the young girl said yes, then the marriage was arranged. If she said no, the young man knew that he had been turned down.

Southeastern families made time to have fun together. Men, women, and children alike would gather around a post in the village center to play a game called postball. The women were given the advantage of being able to use their hands. The men had to use sticks, similar to those used in lacrosse. The object of the game was to hit the post with a ball. After the game was over, everyone would share a festive meal and dance.

Taino families enjoyed having fun, too. Taino parents allowed their children to have parrots as pets. Together, families watched and participated in recreational wrestling matches, foot races, and archery contests. Singing, swimming, and dancing were other ways that Taino families entertained themselves in their tropical homeland. Ꙅ

31

The interior of a Mandan home is shown in this drawing from the 1840s. The Mandan were a tribe of Native Americans that lived on the prairies when the first European settlers arrived in the West.

Buffalo Hunters, Sheep Herders, and Desert Farmers

The tribes of the American West are a diverse lot, ranging from the Native Americans of the Great Plains like the Sioux and Pawnee to the pueblo-dwelling Hopi and Zuñi of the southwest. There were some similarities in family relationships among these many tribal groups, however.

The Hopi were bound by the family ties of 12 clan groups. Called *phratries*, these 12 main clans have many smaller clans within them. Men have always been Hopi religious leaders, but children inherit the clan of their mother. Hopi mothers, daughters, and granddaughters lived together with their children and husbands in one-room homes that were built side by side or atop the one-room dwellings of other Hopi families. The Spanish called these adobe apartment-style complexes "pueblos."

Hopi women made clay pottery for their families, wove baskets from various plants, harvested edible wild plants, and did the cooking. They also maintained the family home, continually smoothing the adobe walls to keep them from weakening due to *erosion*. Hopi men farmed and hunted. They wove cotton for use in blankets and clothing. A Hopi man even made his wife's wedding outfit for her.

The men of Hopi communities belonged to special religious groups that met in **kivas**. They dressed as spirits called kachinas for religious ceremonies. Hopi men, dressed as kachinas, rewarded or disciplined Hopi children based on each child's behavior. Uncles were also the family disciplinarians.

Although they did not do the farming, Hopi women owned the crops farmed by their men. Hopi women also owned their houses, but were only allowed in kivas when invited by the men. Hopi mothers raised both their sons and daughters until the age of six, when the boys were taken into the company of the village men.

Hopi girls had a special squash-blossom hairstyle that announced to the world that they were young women, eligible to marry. A young Hopi maiden had to earn the right to wear this special hairstyle. In order to do so, she participated in a coming-of-age ritual. During part of this ceremony, the young girl had to demonstrate her skill at grinding corn. If she successfully completed her coming-of-age ceremony, she was no longer regarded as a child.

Another tribe of the southwest was the Apache. They were more likely to wander than were the Hopi. Apache men were responsible for hunting and for protecting the family. In some tribal groups, Apache men also were responsible for providing farm labor for their in-laws. The men sometimes dressed up like gans, or mountain spirits, in order to ward off evil spirits, cure illness, or to ask these special spirits to watch over their crops and game.

Most Apache men had only one wife. However, if a man decided to have a second wife, she would usually be one of his first wife's sisters or cousins. He could bring this second wife into the **wickiup** where his first wife lived, or build a second wickiup for his new wife.

A Hidatsa woman grinds grain inside of a building made of wooden beams.

Apache women gathered wood for their extended families, worked together to prepare feasts, gathered acorns, picked mulberries, and collected pine nuts. They made tools, clothing, and baskets for their families. After contact with Europeans, they started sheep herding and passed this skill onto their daughters. They taught their children respect for their elders, the land, and the sacred religious traditions of the Apache nation.

Apache boys had to learn all of the many skills necessary for participation in their band's gathering, hunting, and raiding parties. They usually began war training around the age of 10. Over the course of their pre-teen and early teenage years, Apache boys were taught the qualities and skills of a wise and honorable Apache father, husband, and warrior.

NATIVE AMERICAN LIFE

This photograph shows the famous Sioux medicine man Sitting Bull with his family in front of their home. Sitting Bull was an influential Sioux leader during the 19th century. He opposed the invasion of white settlers into tribal lands, especially the Black Hills of South Dakota, which the Sioux considered a sacred place. Sitting Bull took part in many battles, including the battle of the Little Bighorn where the Sioux and Cheyenne won a great victory over the U.S. 7th Cavalry. After the Sioux were forced to stop fighting and move to a reservation, Sitting Bull traveled throughout the country, asking the government to respect the rights of his people. He was killed in December 1890.

Like the Apache, the tribes living on the Great Plains were nomadic. Until the late 19th century, most Plains tribes traveled through their territories following the buffalo herds. Men of the Plains spent much of their lives in pursuit of buffalo. The buffalo was the source of food, shelter, and clothing for their people, and these men had to be brave, skillful hunters to bring down such large game animals. When they were not hunting, Plains men were kept busy making tools and weapons to help them hunt and protect their families. Although they spent much time away from home, when they were home, Plains fathers were often playful and loving.

Women of the Plains tribes were responsible for child rearing, tepee construction, and transportation. They did the cooking and processed buffalo into dried and fresh meat, storage containers, blankets, tools, clothing, tepee covers, and other essential items. They were also responsible for repairing and maintaining both summer and winter camps. Tepees generally belonged to women.

Beautifully decorated clothing given to Lakota Sioux family members was and still is a sign of affection and respect from wives, mothers, sisters, and grandmothers. Lakota women were quite accomplished in quillwork. The women converted porcupine quills into elaborate decorations for clothing and personal items.

37

Blackfoot fathers taught their daughters how to be proper ladies. They would spend a great deal of time telling their daughters jokes and silly stories over and over again. When their daughters could listen to their teasing and joking without giggling like silly little girls, their fathers praised them generously.

In Hupa villages, women were the healers. They were paid for their services, but only retained their fees if their treatments were successful. Hupa healers were highly regarded within their village social structures. They were often wealthy, and Hupa social standing was based upon wealth.

In many of the families throughout the Plains area, mothers and daughters were quite close. Because mothers had so much work to do processing buffalo meat and hides, grandmothers often oversaw the education of young girls. These honored elder women taught their young granddaughters all the skills necessary to become a respected wife, mother, and adult family member. Grandmothers also taught their granddaughters the tribe's moral values, history, and traditions.

The organization of families differed from tribe to tribe. For example, the Omahas were organized into 10 *paternal* clans, while the Blackfoot were *bilateral*. This meant a Blackfoot could trace his or her lineage through both sides of the family. A Blackfoot woman generally joined her husband's band upon marriage. Like other tribes, chiefs led the extended Skidi Pawnee families. The chief's sons usually followed in his footsteps and became family leaders after their fathers' deaths. Unlike the Blackfoot tribe, however, once a young Pawnee man married he lived in the earth lodge of his wife's family.

The tribes of the Great Plains also had different traditions of courting—what we would call dating today. Courting with blankets

On the Great Plains, the men of the tribe were responsible for hunting buffalo. This animal provided the tribe with meat for food. The buffalo's hide could be used to make clothing, blankets, or tepee coverings and its bones could be made into tools. Women of the tribe dried the meat and prepared the skins, as this 19th–century photograph shows. The women in the center and on the right have staked out the hides and are beating them with sticks as they dry in the sun.

Hopi women check on a meal they
are baking in an adobe oven.

was part of the Cheyenne lifestyle. A single girl who was of age might
stand in front of her family tepee wrapped in a blanket. Young men
who were attracted to her would stand in line for a chance to enter
the blanket with her. The young girl would invite the man of her
choice to stand with her inside the folds of the blanket. There, they
would stand face to face, sharing a few innocent moments together.

A young Sioux man who was interested in a young woman
might attempt to win her favor by playing love songs for her on a
flute. He could also use the flute to send her special, secret messages

that were in a code only he and his beloved understood. If she indicated that she was interested in him, the young man might begin to pursue her more openly.

The parents of a Cora groom would make a number of ritual requests to the bride's parents. The bride's parents could then accept or decline the marriage proposal. The Cora people also gave their young adults a form of premarital counseling. Elders from the family relayed marital advice of the ancestors to the couple in a ceremonial meeting.

Children living in the southwest played a variety of games. One shared by several tribes was a game of skill that involved a hoop and some darts. A player would roll a hoop across the ground as fast as he or she could. Other players would try to throw darts through the moving hoop. Each player had different-colored darts to make keeping score easier.

Southwest girls and boys often played running games. Kick ball was played, and contests in relay racing were often held between villages, tribes, or bands. Sometimes, different villages staged races during which gambling and feasting took place. The racers often ran distances of up to 25 miles.

Plains families sometimes played shinny. This was a game that used special sticks and a small ball. It was played much like modern-day field hockey. Young boys were also expected to practice with their bows, lances, and other weapons so that they would become good hunters and help provide food for the tribe one day. ⑤

5 Families of Abundance and Subsistence

The Native Americans who lived in what today are the northwestern United States and Canada had very diverse lifestyles. The Northwest was a land of abundance. The people living here did not have to work as hard as the natives living in the far north. The Arctic and subarctic regions, on the other hand, were areas in which farming was impossible and survival was difficult.

Traditionally, bilateral extended families formed the basis of most Arctic Inuit societies. Although Inuit society was primarily arranged around the nuclear family, the Inuits also maintained close relationships with their extended family members.

These Athabaskan parents stand proudly behind their children, who hold up the otters they have trapped. Family life was especially important to the Native Americans of the far north.

Nuclear and extended families often lived together. If they did not share the same winter sod home or summer caribou-skin tent, they often lived close to one another in small communities. Individual survival in the Arctic regions was dependent upon the cooperative contributions of all family members, especially during whaling season.

Above all else, Inuit men needed to be hunters and fishermen of the highest quality. Life in the Arctic depended upon stockpiling foods such as whale, seal, caribou, and arctic *char*. In coastal whaling villages, whaling captains were highly respected and admired. In villages that did not whale, the best hunters were held in high regard. Respected and admired above all Inuit men, however, was the family shaman.

The Inuit shaman possessed a gift for contacting spirits. He was also a wise man, able to instruct his people in times of trouble. The Inuit shaman was a healer and teacher who had great knowledge of

Women of the northwestern tribes were well known for the watertight baskets they wove from grasses and plants, as well as their for beautifully decorated wooden boxes. The boxes were so finely fitted together that they could be used to cook food. Very hot rocks were put into the box around or under the food. The box was then closed and the food was left to cook in this small wooden oven. The tighter the box was fit together, the more heat it would hold in and the better it would cook food.

Members of an Inuit family sit down together for a meal. Traditionally, the Inuit maintained close relationships with both immediate and extended family members.

humans, animals, and the spirits. A good shaman knew many herbal remedies and other types of treatments for illnesses.

Inuit women of the Arctic were mothers, wives, homemakers, and gatherers. They kept track of the family food supplies. They sewed fine

This painting of Inuit snow cottages, also called igloos, was made around 1834 by a man who had sailed with Captain James Ross's polar expedition. Ross was a 19th century English explorer who traveled to both the Arctic and Antarctic regions. After returning from the Arctic in 1833, he described how the Inuit people he met lived.

fur parkas to keep their husbands and children warm. They sewed seal- and walrus-gut raincoats to keep their husbands and sons dry during whale and seal hunting season. They collected salmonberries and other edible tundra plants in the late spring, summer, and early fall.

Inuit children were often adopted out of large families and into smaller ones. This was done so that they would receive the amount of food, shelter, attention, and clothing necessary for survival in the harsh environment of their homeland. Children who were adopted into another family often grew up knowing both sets of parents. As this was an accepted and understood practice, they did not feel ashamed or unwanted because of their adopted status.

An Inuit girl who was fully grown exchanged the clothes of her childhood for those of an adult woman. In some Inuit groups, she was also tattooed to mark her status as an adult. Inuit boys also changed their style of dress when they became recognized as grown men.

When an Inuit boy was deemed ready for marriage, two slits were cut in his cheeks or near the corners of his mouth. Ivory or bone cheek or lip plugs were placed in the openings. These cheek plugs visually announced to all that the boy was now a man, eligible for marriage.

Another people of the Arctic were the Aleut, who lived in the far northwest. The Aleut traced their family relatives through their mother's family bloodlines. Aleut society had hereditary classes of high nobles, commoners, and slaves. The leaders were recruited from the high nobles' class. They lived in communal homes called *barabaras*.

47

GAMES OF THE NORTH

Native American children who lived in the Far North and Northwest played a variety of games. In some areas of the Arctic children played a game called "polar bear." One child pretended to be a sleeping old lady. Another pretended to be her sleeping child. The "polar bear" snuck up to them and took away the sleeping child. The "child" had to hide wherever the "polar bear" put him or her. The "old lady" was then awakened and had to search for her child.

Inuit kick-ball was played with a stuffed ball made from caribou or other animal skin. Two teams opposed each other and tried to maintain control of the ball. There were no goals like in soccer, but the game resembled modern-day soccer in many other ways.

Story telling was another form of Inuit entertainment. At night, when the family was safe inside their home, a father would entertain his children and wife with tales from his life or the lives of his ancestors. During this special family time, he would share stories that taught his children the history of their people, the values of their culture, and the teachings of their religion.

Northwest boys competed against each other in foot races, archery contests, and wrestling matches. The girls played with carved wooden dolls. Both girls and boys swam and played on the beaches.

In comparison to the subsistence families of these other regions, the people of the Northwest lived in relative splendor.

The Northwest Haida were divided into two phratries: the Raven and the Eagle. Each of these was divided into a large number of clans. One or more clans formed a village. Haida clans were matrilineal.

Boys and girls alike played a game much like modern-day horseshoes. Stakes were driven into the ground at opposite ends of a playing field. The players tossed roots at these stakes and tried to see who could land their root closest to the stake.

Families in the subarctic culture region played a game that was similar to the shell game. Players would each be given an equal number of tokens or markers of some sort. A player would take one token and then with both hands out of his or her opponent's view, place it in one hand. Now, he or she would display two clenched fists. The opponent would guess in which hand the token was being held. If he or she guessed correctly, the prize was the marker. When one player ran out of markers, the other player was declared the winner.

Young Sanpoil girls of the plateau area played with dolls. They made these dolls by sticking clay balls atop sticks and wrapping them in bits of animal skin. The boys played with tops that were made from available local hardwoods. Sanpoil girls and boys turned somersaults, practiced walking on their hands, and did handstands. Their parents liked to play gambling games. Entire families enjoyed playing several games of skill that used hoops and poles.

Haida men's titles and wealth were inherited through the mother's side of the family. Men, however, owned the houses in Haida society. The fathers' clans built these wooden-plank longhouses. When a man died, his sister's eldest son inherited his house.

Haida clan chiefs were men. All of the clan chiefs of a village would be members of a council. The wealthiest clan chief was recognized as the village chief.

Haida marriages were often arranged. The two parties who were to be married had to be from different clans. They also were expected to be from the same social class. Sometimes, marriages were arranged when the husband- and wife-to-be were still small children. Unless one of the two children disgraced themselves or their families, they would usually be married to their arranged spouse when they came of age.

If a Haida man neglected or abused his wife, her parents had the right to take her and their grandchildren away from him. If he left his wife for another woman, then he was forced to pay reparations to his first wife. If he refused, he was punished severely, sometimes by death. However, if there was no other woman involved, a Haida man could leave his wife and family without fear of retribution.

Another tribe of the Northwest was the Cayuse. In this tribe men and boys hunted for food and to provide hides for clothing. They also provided their people with animal bones and antlers for making tools and utensils. Elk, deer, bear, antelope, and mountain sheep were hunted across their north-central North American homeland. The Cayuse men were accomplished hunters who learned to be comfortable hunting with bows, spears, knives, nets, and traps. Cayuse men also fished for salmon. This was often done from shore, using long-handled dip nets. The nets were used to reach out into the rushing streams and capture salmon that were swimming upstream to spawn.

Cayuse women cleaned salmon and hung them on long racks to dry in the sun. They dug for roots using wooden or bone digging tools. They mashed roots together and shaped them into little balls to make small sun-dried biscuits. When there was time, the Cayuse women took their children into the mountains to go berry picking. There they would pick huckleberries for drying. They also picked chokecherries to mix with dried meat or fish to make *pemmican*.

Children of the Salish tribe, which lived on the coast of North America, spent a lot of time with their grandparents while their parents were hunting, fishing, or gathering food. In fact, grandparents were the primary teachers. They taught family history, as well as the qualities and skills the young Salish children would need to be a good member of their society. §

The members of this family are Maya Indians
of Central America. Around 1,600 years ago,
their ancestors established a highly evolved
society in Mexico and Central America. Today
Mayan families still follow some of the same
practices of the ancient Maya.

Family Ties in Central and South America

Before the arrival of Europeans during the 16th century in the region today called Latin America, two of the major native groups were the Maya of Mexico and Central America and the Inca of South America.

The Inca of South America had a hierarchical, patriarchal class structure. Men were the heads of their families and of the Incan society. Families were divided into classes. The ruling class was composed of the ruler and his family members. Temple priests, architects, and regional army commanders were lower in class only to the elite members of the ruling-class family. The two lowest classes were made of artisans, soldiers, and peasant farmers. These farmers grew all of the crops necessary to feed their own families, as well as the families of the upper classes.

Ruling-class women sometimes had power, but it was more usual for rulers to be men. The sapa (high priest or ruler) and the army commander were the most important men in any Incan village.

Inca women used llama wool and cotton to weave cloth. Dyes were made from indigo and other plants. The finest dyed and woven cloths were given to the ruling class. A particularly fine weaving might

Both the Inca and Maya enjoyed a special ball game. Most cities had ball courts close to their centers, and ball games were a big event. To play, two teams faced off on the ball court. The players could not touch the ball with their hands—they could only use elbows, knees, or hips. The players scored by touching special markers or passing the ball through their team's ring.

be given to the gods during an important religious ceremony. Cloth was also used as a material for bartering. Fine cloth might be traded for cocoa, turkey, or even gold.

Inca children did not always live long lives. Sometimes, they were chosen to serve as sacrifices to the Sun God. These children were taken high into the mountains and buried alive with food, corn beer, and coca leaves during annual ceremonies that were held to ensure a good harvest and a happy Sun God. To be chosen to serve as a sacrifice was considered to be a great honor.

Inca men were expected to marry by the age of 20. Brides and grooms would exchange sandals at their wedding ceremonies. Inca leaders married their sisters to keep the blood of their families pure. Their sisters became their first, or principal, wives. The Inca tradition was for the son of the ruler and his principal wife, or sister, to be the heir to the throne.

Like the Inca, the Maya of Central America also had a family-based *caste* system. Caste membership was hereditary. The elite noble class was made up of the ruler, his family, nobles, and priests. Upon the death of a

AGOSTO
CHACRAIAPVI
quilla

tiempo de labransa — haylli mi ynca
ha ra

Inca men loosen the soil with a *taccla* (foot-plow), while women behind them sow seeds in this drawing from an Inca codex. The book, which dates to 1565, is the only codex in existence that shows drawings of 16th-century Peruvian life.

ruler, his son or brother took his place. Mayans who were not born into the elite noble class were divided into a class of warriors, a middle class of tradesmen and craftsmen, or a lower-class peasantry.

Mayan working-class men were skilled tradesmen. The peasant men were farmers. They spent most of their days in the fields. They grew maize (corn), cotton, beans, squash, and cacao. Mayan peasant women were often skilled weavers as well. They used cotton to weave cloth. The dyes used by Mayan women included indigo, brazil wood, logwood, annatto, and iron oxide. They also made baskets.

Soon after birth, a Mayan infant's head was pressed between two boards. It was secured and left this way for several days. The pressure

If an Inca child went to school, the child was taught to make and read the Inca *quipu*. A *quipu* was made of many colored knots tied together. The way that the knots were spaced and the colors of the cotton rope used to make them all had special meanings. Religion, law, and math were also studied.

reshaped the child's skull. It is believed that this was done to make the shape of the head resemble that of an ear of corn.

Upper-class Mayan children were taught to read and write using pictograms and hieroglyphics. They studied religion, math, and astronomy. They also studied the Mayan calendar and learned to count and write out the Mayan numeral system.

When Mayan boys and girls became teenagers, they participated in a celebration called the "Descent of the Gods." After this, a matchmaker could negotiate their marriages. The bride's father expected to receive a good price for his young daughter's hand in marriage. The bridegroom's father would try to negotiate a fair amount of time for his son to work for his father-in-law. After the marriage, the husband would have to work for his wife's parents for five to six years. ⑤

Chronology

Before 10,000 B.C. Paleo-Indians migrate from parts of Asia and begin settling throughout the Americas.

10,000–5000 B.C. Medicine-wheel spiritual sites are built in the Great Basin region.

6000–5000 B.C. The subarctic regions are settled as the climate begins to warm with the waning of the last Ice Age.

5000–3000 B.C. Earliest-known organized Native American settlements are built in the Southeast.

1400 B.C.–A.D. 1500 Northeastern woodland cultures rise and prosper.

A.D. 300–900 Maya civilization reaches its highest point.

300 Native Americans begin settling in the Plains region and migrating with the buffalo herds and the seasons of the year.

1400–1521 The Aztecs dominate Mesoamerica.

1492–1502 Columbus explores the West Indies and Central America.

1740–1780 European wars in the Northeast severely affect lifestyles of Native Americans in this region.

1760–1848 Growing Spanish influence around California begins to have impact on the lives of Native Americans in this region; missionaries begin attempts to "civilize" and "Christianize" Native Americans of this area.

1830 Congress passes the Indian Removal Act, calling for Native Americans living east of the Mississippi River to be moved to a government-established Indian Territory located in what is present-day Oklahoma.

1838 Cherokee are forced to move from the Southeast to Oklahoma on the "Trail of Tears."

1887 The Dawes/General Allotment Act divides reservations into 80- and 160-acre tracts; these land parcels are to be owned by individual Indians.

1952 Federal Relocation Policy is passed; this policy seeks to terminate all government services for Native Americans, negate treaty agreements, and relocate Native Americans from reservations to inner cities.

1971 Congress passes Alaska Native Claims Settlement Act.

1972 "Trail of Broken Treaties" organized by AIM results in a weeklong occupation of the Bureau of Indian Affairs headquarters in Washington, D.C.

1992 This year marks the 500th anniversary of Columbus' entry to the West Indies, prompting many Native American artists to create artwork expressing their feelings about Columbus and subsequent Europeans and their effects upon the Native American culture.

2003 Recent census figures indicate that there are more than 3 million Native Americans living in the United States and Canada.

Glossary

acclimate to adapt to a new temperature, altitude, climate, environment, or situation.

bilateral having two sides.

breechcloth a cloth worn about the loins or hip area.

cassava a type of melon.

caste a division of society based on differences of wealth, inherited rank or privilege, profession, or occupation.

char a small-scaled trout with light-colored spots.

clan a group of people tracing descent from a common ancestor.

erosion the wearing away of soil, usually by wind or water.

fast to go without food for a period of time.

kiva a ceremonial structure that is usually round and partly underground.

lineage descent in a line from a common progenitor.

longhouse a long communal dwelling.

matrilineal relating to, based on, or tracing descent through the maternal line.

moiety one of two basic complementary tribal subdivisions.

oratorical relating to speaking in public eloquently or effectively.

palisade a fence of stakes designed for defense.

paternal of or relating to the father.

patriarchal characteristic of a social organization marked by the supremacy of the father in the clan or family.

patrilineal relating to, based on, or tracing descent through the paternal line.

pemmican a concentrated food consisting of lean meat dried, pounded fine, and mixed with melted fat.

sagamore a subordinate chief of the Algonquian Indians of the North Atlantic coast.

totem an object serving as the emblem of a family or clan and often as a reminder of its ancestry.

vision quest a personal spiritual search undertaken by an adolescent Native American boy in order to learn the identity of his guardian spirit.

wickiup a hut with a usually oval base and a rough frame covered with reed mats, grass, or brushwood.

wigwam a hut having typically an arched framework of poles overlaid with bark, rush mats, or hides.

Further Reading

Carew-Miller, Anna. *Native American Confederacies*. Philadelphia: Mason Crest
Publishers, 2003.

Hoxie, Frederick E. *Encyclopedia of the North American Indians*. New York:
Houghton Mifflin, 1996.

Moulton, Candy. *Everyday Life Among the American Indians*. Cincinnati:
Writer's Digest Books, 2001.

Pritzker, Barry M. *A Native American Encyclopedia: History, Culture, and
Peoples*. New York: Oxford University Press, 2000.

Internet Resources

http://www.channel-e-philadelphia.com/nattopics.html
The Native American Timeline Web site includes timeframes, topics,
resources, and a discussion forum for all sorts of information pertaining to
Native Americans.

http://www.nativeweb.org/resources/
This Web site features a collection of resources and links to informative
Native American Web sites.

http://www.si.edu/resource/faq/nmai/start.htm
This site contains fascinating information collected by the Smithsonian
Institution about Native American history and culture.

http://www.ilt.columbia.edu/k12/naha/natime.html
This is a timeline of Native American history and includes information on
various events.

Index

Picture Credits

3: Corbis
8: David and Peter Turnley/Corbis
10: Corbis
12: Nathan Benn/Corbis
15: Jim Richardson/Corbis
16: AINACO/Corbis
22: Corbis
25: (top) © OTTN Publishing; (bottom) Library of Congress
26: Hulton/Archive/Getty Images
29: Hulton/Archive/Getty Images
32: Historical Picture Archive/Corbis
35: Richard A. Cooke/Corbis
36: Library of Congress

39: (top) Hulton/Archive/Getty Images; (bottom) Bettmann/Corbis
40: Bettmann/Corbis
42: Joel Bennett/Corbis
45: Richard A. Cooke/Corbis
46: Hulton/Archive/Getty Images
52: Jeremy Horner/Corbis
55: Werner Forman/Art Resource, NY

Cover credits:
front) Smithsonian American Art Museum, Washington, D.C./Art Resource, NY
(back) Craig Aurness/Corbis

Contributors

Dr. Troy Johnson is a Professor of American Indian Studies and History at California State University, Long Beach, California. He is an internationally published author and is the author, co-author, or editor of fifteen books, including *Contemporary Political Issues of the American Indian* (1999), *Red Power: The American Indians' Fight for Freedom* (1999), *American Indian Activism: Alcatraz to the Longest Walk* (1997), and *The Occupation of Alcatraz Island: Indian Self-Determination and the Rise of Indian Activism* (1996). He has published numerous scholarly articles, has spoken at conferences across the United States, and is a member of the editorial board of the journals *American Indian Culture and Research* and *The History Teacher.* Dr. Johnson has served as president of the Society of History Education since 2001. He has been profiled in *Reference Encyclopedia of the American Indian* (2000) and *Directory of American Scholars* (2000). He has won awards for his permanent exhibit at Alcatraz Island; he also was named Most Valuable Professor of the Year by California State University, Long Beach, in 1997. He served as associate director and historical consultant on the PBS documentary film *Alcatraz Is Not an Island* (1999), which won first prize at the 26th annual American Indian Film Festival and was screened at the Sundance Film Festival in 2001. Dr. Johnson lives in Long Beach, California.

Colleen Madonna Flood Williams is the wife of Paul R. Williams, mother of Dillon Joseph Meehan, and daughter of Patrick and Kathleen Flood. She lives in Alaska with her husband, son, and their dog, Kosmos Kramer. She has a bachelor's degree in elementary education with a minor in art.